A Royal Cookbook

A ROYAL COOKBOOK

Seasonal recipes from Buckingham Palace

Mark Flanagan and Edward Griffiths

ROYAL COLLECTION TRUST

CONTENTS

FOREWORD

EDWARD GRIFFITHS

The ultimate experience of a great meal comes from the marriage of exquisite cuisine and the delivery of professional yet personal service. Neither element is more important than the other, for success lies in the combination of a well-planned and well-executed menu, thoughtful presentation in attractive dishes, and service at a beautifully laid table by a highly trained team of staff. This philosophy is as important to the Royal Household as it is to other great establishments known for their food and service.

Yet, essentially, the heart of the pleasure is simple: excellent food amidst a beautiful setting. And this is where this book comes in, for such a combination can be achieved by anyone – through the use of quality ingredients and an inspired approach to the table.

A Royal Cookbook is organised along broadly seasonal lines, because a commitment to seasonal produce is the foundation of cookery in the royal kitchens. Royal menus today are a far cry from the roast swan and turtle soup of the past; based largely on French classical cuisine, they continue to evolve and are adapted to match contemporary trends. We hope that some of the ingredients in these recipes will encourage you to rediscover your local butchers, fishmongers or market (although where possible, viable alternatives for less easy-to-source ingredients have been suggested). The royal kitchens look to the various residences for much of their supplies: meats from the farm at Windsor; game from the Highlands surrounding Balmoral; fruits from the orchards at Sandringham; and herbs and honey from the garden at Buckingham Palace.

A table set for lunch in the splendour of the White Drawing Room, Buckingham Palace.

The Royal Household is also blessed with historic collections of fine porcelain, silver gilt and crystal, which add to the splendid interiors of the palaces and residences. This book takes the opportunity to use some of these magnificent pieces in illustrating the recipes, whilst also providing tips and suggestions on how to translate such presentation into practical creativity for your home. Also included are explanations of table settings, floral arrangements and other adornments, to inspire your own approach.

The menus that follow have been carefully selected to work in the domestic kitchen, with minimal use of specialist equipment. These dishes can mostly be prepared well in advance – leaving you free to relax and enjoy that other key element in a wonderful meal: good company.

The Rhubarb and White Chocolate Parfait on a plate from the Staffordshire Minton Dessert Service, made for Queen Victoria in 1879. The recipe for this dish is given on page 64.

A History of Royal Dining

'The Kitchens at the royal establishments, particularly those at Windsor Castle, were vastly superior in every way … I remember on my first day at Windsor thinking how much the kitchen reminded me of a chapel with its high domed ceiling, its feeling of airiness and light and the gleam of copper, well-worn and burnished, at each end of the room.'

Gabriel Tschumi, *Royal Chef: Forty Years with the Royal Households*, 1954

ABOVE: James Stephanoff, *The Kitchen at Windsor Castle*, 1817.
LEFT: The Kitchen at Windsor Castle, 1878.

ABOVE: Alexander Creswell, *The Great Kitchen at Windsor Castle after the restorations following the fire*, 1999.

The Great Kitchen at Windsor Castle is the oldest working kitchen in England; medieval oak beams still support its arching roof. This space has been serving up dishes for kings, queens and commoners since the days of Edward III, around 1360, and although modern appliances have taken the place of some of the old ranges and open fires, many of the tables, workbenches and shelves still date back some two hundred years. Guests at the Castle might eat food which has bubbled up over the ciphers of George IV and Queen Victoria, branded into still-shining copper pans. The Great Kitchen embodies the combination of the historical and the contemporary that is the continuing theme of royal dining.

The kitchens at the royal residences have seen monarchs, chefs and food fashions come and go. They served Charles I when he dined 'in public' (or rather in full view of his courtiers), served only on bended knee, supplied 'ice cream' for the first

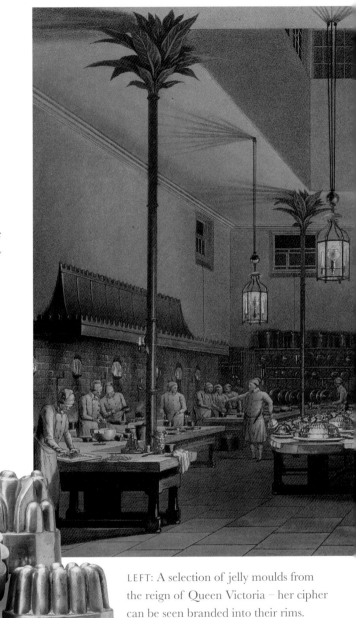

LEFT: A selection of jelly moulds from the reign of Queen Victoria – her cipher can be seen branded into their rims.

Gabriel Tschumi, whilst still a young apprentice at the Royal Household.

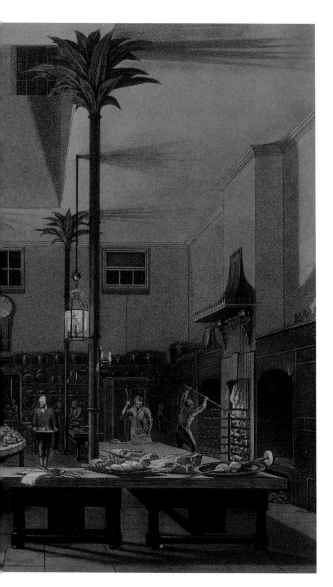

ABOVE: James Tingle, *Marie Antoine Carême, chef to the Prince Regent, giving directions in the kitchens of Brighton Pavilion*, 1838.

recorded time in England for the Garter Banquet of Charles II in 1671, and sent up dishes to a dinner table decorated with a running stream and live fish in the time of the Prince Regent. The latter's coronation banquet in Westminster Hall upon becoming George IV was a display of unparalleled extravagance: amongst the thousands of dishes served to guests were some 160 tureens of soup, 480 sauceboats, 80 dishes of 'daubed geese' and 400 jellies and creams. Even the grandest State Banquet today is a rather more restrained affair, with around 170 guests enjoying a three-course meal.

Over the centuries, several famous chefs have headed the kitchens: in 1816 the Prince Regent invited the French chef Marie Antoine Carême to serve him at Brighton. Disappointed by the English chefs' overuse of pepper, amongst other practices, Carême returned to the continent after only six months. Queen Victoria also looked to Europe for her cooks, employing the Swiss Gabriel Tschumi, whilst King Edward VII not only employed a French chef (Henri Cédard) but also an Egyptian, whose specific role was to make Turkish coffee for royal dinner parties.

The setting and decoration of the dining table have also evolved over the centuries, although the use of the finest gold and silver has always been a mark of royal dining. As cooks and their kitchens became more sophisticated, so did the table decorations. In Tudor times whole peacocks would be plucked, roasted and then re-feathered for display. The late eighteenth and early nineteenth centuries witnessed a fashion for ornate edible decorations: even the modest-living George III's banquets had decorations such as 'temples four feet high, in which the different stories were sweetmeats', whilst Carême's table adornments for the King's son included edible architectural follies and ruins. The display of a 'buffet' of gold and silver is however one aspect of the feast which has remained constant through several reigns up to the present day; historically an impressive show of status, it is now only used only on the occasion of state banquets.

LEFT: Silver-gilt plateau with Bacchanalian dining figures, part of the table setting for a State Banquet.

RIGHT: Joseph Nash, *Queen Victoria and Louis-Philippe of France entering St George's Hall, 11 October 1844*, 1844. A large display of a buffet is visible, dominating the far end of the Hall in Windsor Castle.

BELOW: A twenty-first-century display of silver-gilt in the Ballroom at Buckingham Palace.

The State Banquet held at Buckingham Palace to celebrate the visit of the US President, Barack Obama, 24 May 2011.

There is even a history of previous royal cookbooks, beginning with *The Forme of Cury*, written by a master cook to Richard II (reigned 1377–99). This is testament to the already sophisticated style of cookery employed within the royal household – ingredients for a salad include parsley, sage, garlic, onions, leek, borage, mint, fennel, cress, rue, rosemary and purslane, and other recipes include parsnip and apple fritters, pears cooked in red wine and ginger, and blancmange.

In 1710 a new royal cookbook was published, produced from the papers of Patrick Lamb, whose biography describes him as 'Near 50 Years Master Chef to their late Majesties King Charles II, King James II, King William and Queen Mary, and to Her Present Majesty Queen Anne'. *Royal Cookery; or, the Complete Court-Cook* even includes a recipe for 'Chicken surprize'.

'The hour of the Meals being come, and all things are now in a readiness, le Maistre Hostel takes a clean Napkin, folded at length, but narrow, and throws it over his Shoulder, remembring that this is … a particular sign and demonstration of his Office; … he must not be shamefaced, nor so much as blush, no not before any noble Personage … for he may do his Office with his Sword by his side, his Cloak upon his Shoulders, and his Hat on his Head, but his Napkin must be always upon his Shoulder …'

From *A perfect School of INSTRUCTIONS For the Officers of the Mouth* … by 'Giles Rose one of the Master Cooks in His Majesties Kitchen' (London, 1682).

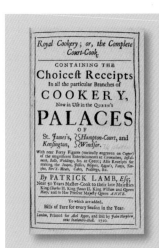

TO MAKE AN ALMOND-TART.
Raise an excellent Paſte, fix corners, and an Inch deep, and take ſome blanch'd Almonds, very finely beaten with Roſe-Water; take a Pound of Sugar to a Pound of Almonds, ſome grated Bread, Nutmeg, a little Cream, with ſtrain'd Spinnage, as much as will colour the Almonds green. So bake it with a gentle, hot Oven, not ſhutting the Door. Draw it, and ſtick it with Orange-Citron.

THE RECIPE BOOK OF MILDRED NICHOLLS, KITCHEN MAID

Mildred Dorothy Nicholls joined the Royal Household in 1908, in the position of seventh kitchen maid. By the time she left to be married in 1919 she had become third kitchen maid. The royal kitchens at the time were divided into sections with different specialities; it seems from the recipes she wrote into this notebook that Mildred's role was to assist the pastry chef. These pages show that the dishes prepared in the kitchens were not only destined for royal tables – opposite the recipe for 'The Royal's plum pudding' is another version, 'Servants Plum Pudding'. Other recipes in the book include a favourite dish of Queen Alexandra, the Danish pudding 'Rodgröd', and 'HM the Queen's recipe' for Bath buns, 'sent down Sunday Jan 2 1910'.

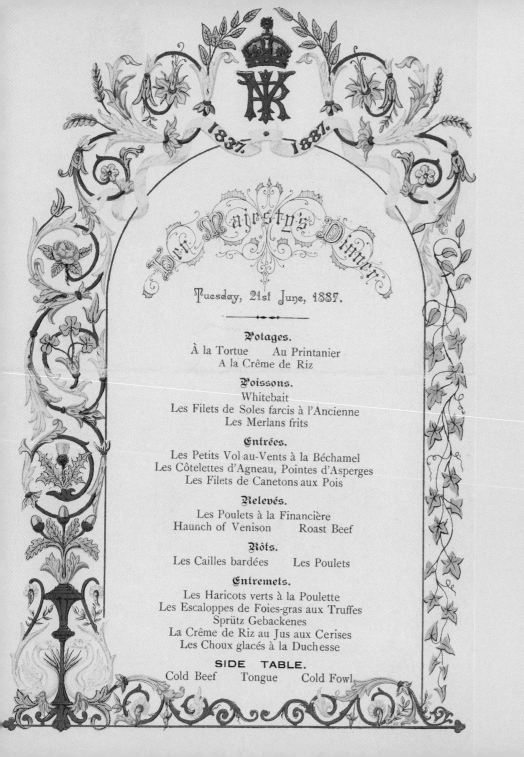

Her Majesty's Dinner

Tuesday, 21st June, 1887.

Potages.
À la Tortue   Au Printanier
A la Crême de Riz

Poissons.
Whitebait
Les Filets de Soles farcis à l'Ancienne
Les Merlans frits

Entrées.
Les Petits Vol-au-Vents à la Béchamel
Les Côtelettes d'Agneau, Pointes d'Asperges
Les Filets de Canetons aux Pois

Relevés.
Les Poulets à la Financière
Haunch of Venison   Roast Beef

Rôts.
Les Cailles bardées   Les Poulets

Entremets.
Les Haricots verts à la Poulette
Les Escaloppes de Foies-gras aux Truffes
Sprütz Gebackenes
La Crême de Riz au Jus aux Cerises
Les Choux glacés à la Duchesse

SIDE TABLE.
Cold Beef   Tongue   Cold Fowl

Menu of Queen Victoria's Jubilee dinner, 21 June 1887. The dishes featured on this menu, and on that pictured opposite, are all written in French – a tradition that continues with royal menus to this day.

The royal kitchens today have been shaped by centuries of history, innovation, personal preferences and public performances. Centuries-old utensils sit alongside cutting-edge appliances; guests of the present day can be served from porcelain, silverware and glassware once owned and used by illustrious figures of the past. Many of the dishes, including some of those featured in this book, have been handed down through generations of royal chefs.

Menu of Queen Victoria's dinner, 14 May 1874, featuring an illustration of Windsor Castle.

THE KITCHENS TODAY

More than 50,000 people visit Buckingham Palace each year as The Queen's guests at banquets, lunches, dinners, receptions and garden parties, with numerous more attending events at Windsor Castle and the Palace of Holyroodhouse in Edinburgh. A team of 20 chefs and sous-chefs caters for all these guests, for members of the Royal Family and for staff of the Royal Households. Even on an ordinary day the kitchens will feed hundreds of people. Menus are changed each week and the chefs travel between the royal residences according to The Queen's schedule, so have to be fully familiar with the arrangements of the different kitchens. The team in the royal kitchens is overseen by the Royal Chef. There is also a Royal Pastry Chef who is responsible for the sweet elements of the menus: puddings, petits fours, cakes and their decorations.

State Banquets are held twice a year, in London or at Windsor. On these magnificent occasions the team of chefs, often with additional help brought in especially for the event, will produce a four-course dinner for up to 250 covers, as well as meals for the remaining Household staff, the orchestra, the pipers, the Yeoman of the Guard, security and medical teams, and drivers.

Preparations for entertaining at the royal residences involve other teams from within the Royal Household. The linen rooms supply damask tablecloths, napkins and doilies. Dining tables will be adorned with seasonal arrangements of flowers, and sometimes decorative piles of fruit. Silverware and glassware come from the silver and glass pantries; these hold items of great beauty and historic significance.

Wine is supplied by the royal cellars, decanted into glass jugs and decanters. Then finally from the kitchens, footmen will deliver the food; pages in dark blue livery serve the guests at the table. Each meal, and the setting in which it is served, is the result of a highly collaborative effort aimed at maintaining the very best standards in hospitality.

Sourcing the Ingredients

Local, seasonal produce is at the heart of cookery in the Royal Household. Even for State Banquets most of the food will be sourced from local suppliers, and wherever possible there is emphasis on British produce. Wonderfully flavoursome beef, pork, lamb and game are all sourced from the Royal Estates, along with a wide variety of home-grown fruits and vegetables.

In the autumn, venison and other game from the Balmoral Estate in Scotland is often on the menu; the population of wild Scottish deer is managed in accordance with conservation laws which support the diverse range of wildlife across the entire Estate. Prized for its distinctive flavour, venison from Balmoral is not reserved solely for royal larders: it can be found in butchers' shops and restaurants across Britain. Balmoral Castle also has a large kitchen garden which provides the Household with fresh fruit, vegetables and flowers (pictured overleaf).

ABOVE: Baskets of onions and shallots for sale in the Windsor Farm Shop.

OPPOSITE: (*Clockwise from top left*) Spring in the apple orchards on the Sandringham Estate; the Victorian dairy in the grounds of Windsor Castle; pigs at Windsor tended to by a specialist pig farmer; rows of lettuces ready for the picking in the Balmoral kitchen garden.

The Sandringham Estate in Norfolk is well known for its apples and apple juice; the orchards were planted by King George V in the 1930s and now produce eight varieties of apples, pressed into juices on site in a traditional Norfolk barn. This apple juice is not only sold locally but again makes its way into shops across the country, and is even served at Buckingham Palace garden parties. The Estate also produces blackcurrants for cordial, and includes arable farmland, growing wheat, rye, parsnips, maize, oats, beans, millet and barley.

Windsor Home Park, to the south of the Castle, has a long history of food production. George III was caricatured as 'Farmer George' for his enthusiastic promotion of agriculture within the Park, whilst decades later Prince Albert, consort of Queen Victoria, helped to design the hothouses that would supply the Household with exotic fruits for over 100 years.

Towards the end of the nineteenth century these abundant greenhouses were producing 4,000 pounds of grapes, 520 dozen peaches, 220 dozen nectarines, 180 dozen apricots, 239 pineapples and 400 melons in a single year. Today the Farm continues to supply its own shop, as well as local outlets, with a range of beef, pork, lamb and poultry.

Buckingham Palace itself has a 16-hectare garden (pictured), and in its very heart can be found a wilderness, now home to a community of bees. In 2009 two hives were introduced into the garden in response to a widespread decline in bee populations; these hives are positioned on an island in the garden's lake, where the bees have access to over 350 different wildflowers. The hives are cared for by a keeper from the London Beekeepers' Association and in their first year alone the two hives produced 83 jars of honey. Since then, two further hives have been added, as well as two on the rooftop of Clarence House.

The recipes in this book feature several ingredients produced by the Royal Estates – Balmoral venison and Windsor lamb – as well as other British delights, such as Arbroath smokies and English asparagus. Whilst the recipes are flexible, with more widely available alternatives suggested wherever possible, the emphasis is always on celebrating local, seasonal produce. By using quality, ethically sourced ingredients in your cooking, you will already be well on your way to serving up a feast.

SUMMER

Crown of Asparagus with Crab and Mango

Paupiette of Sole with Watercress Mousse

Sablé Breton with English Strawberries and Lemon Cream

*Light summer lunches tempt the palate and refresh
the senses while the sun shines. The menu here begins
with a flourish, and ends with a cunning combination
of French patisserie and English strawberries.
In between, a delicate main course of fresh sole
and peppery watercress.*

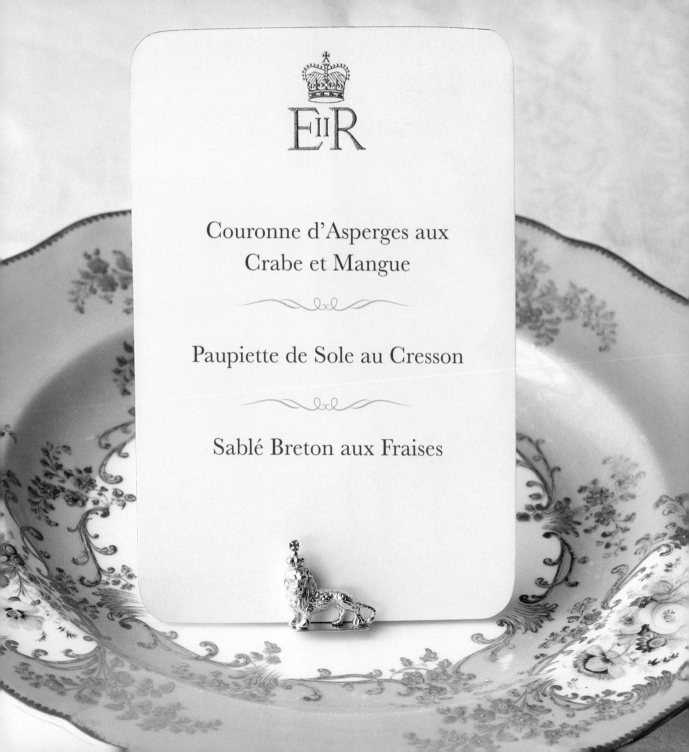

E II R

Couronne d'Asperges aux
Crabe et Mangue

Paupiette de Sole au Cresson

Sablé Breton aux Fraises

SERVES 6

INGREDIENTS
48 pieces of medium asparagus
350g fresh white crabmeat
½ bunch chives
1 ripe Alphonso mango
3 sun-blush tomatoes
zest of 1 lemon
zest of 1 lime
200ml crème fraîche
¼ bunch mizuna leaves (Japanese
    brassica)
¼ bunch rocket leaves
¼ head curly endive (frisée lettuce)

For the lemon dressing:
juice of 1 lemon
juice of 1 lime
1 teaspoon Dijon mustard
100ml walnut oil
salt and pepper

iced water, to refresh the asparagus
    and chives

EQUIPMENT
6 small steel or plastic rings

Crown of Asparagus with Crab and Mango

COURONNE D'ASPERGES AUX CRABE ET MANGUE

A spectacular starter with just a hint of a royal theme, this exquisite little 'crown' holds within it a ravishing combination of light summer flavours.

Using a vegetable peeler, peel the spears of asparagus carefully, leaving 1 cm of green below the tip. Cut off and discard any woody ends.

Cook the spears in boiling salted water, ensuring they are cooked through and tender (not *al dente*); refresh in iced water. Drain and pat dry on a clean cloth.

Cut the spears into 7cm lengths, measured from the tip, and then cut these in half lengthwise. The remaining lower parts of the asparagus should be cut into round slices of 0.5cm thickness and set aside.

Carefully pick through the crabmeat, ensuring there are no small particles of shell remaining. Put into a small bowl and chill.

Blanch 12 chives in boiling water for 5 seconds and then refresh in ice water. Pat the chives dry and tie pairs of leaves together at one end to create 6 long strands ready to wrap around the asparagus crowns.

Peel and dice the mango into 0.5cm pieces. Grate the zest of the lemon and lime. Dice the sun-blush tomatoes. Finely chop the remaining chives. Gently combine the crab, diced mango, chopped tomatoes and asparagus rounds, then add the chives and lemon and lime zest. Bind the mixture together with a little crème fraîche, and season.

Juice the lemon and lime and make a vinaigrette by adding the Dijon mustard, walnut oil and salt and pepper.

TO ASSEMBLE

Stand 16 halves of asparagus inside each ring mould, with the sliced inside of the asparagus spears facing outward. Keep the spears tightly together or else the 'crowns' will open.

Half fill the crown of asparagus with the crab mix, making sure the filling is quite compacted. Allow to set slightly in the fridge for 20 minutes before serving.

Just before you are ready to serve, mix the salad leaves with some of the vinaigrette (reserving a little to drizzle around each plate).

TO SERVE

Put a dessertspoonful of crème fraîche in the middle of each plate and spread it slightly into a pool. Lift a crown of asparagus and crab on to the centre of each plate with a palette knife.

Arrange the round slices of asparagus in a circle around the crown. Slide the ring mould halfway up and, still holding the ring in place (this may require help), tie a length of chive around the crown before lifting the ring off completely. Repeat this for all six crowns.

Fill the top half of each crown with the dressed salad leaves. Arrange any further cubes of mango and small leaves around the plates and drizzle with the remaining vinaigrette.

PRESENTATION

This Crown of Asparagus is presented on a lattice-edged plate from Crown Derby. This particular plate is part of a service dated 1877, which originally came from the Royal Yacht Osborne *and eventually arrived at Buckingham Palace after the decommissioning of the Royal Yacht* Britannia.

Flat plates lend the greatest emphasis to the height of the asparagus crown – serve these in a bowl and some of the effect would undoubtedly be lost.

SERVES 6

INGREDIENTS

14 quarter-cut Dover sole fillets
  (skinless)
1 free-range egg
350ml whipping cream
2 bunches watercress
1 bunch flat parsley
100g baby spinach
salt and pepper

beurre blanc sauce (see recipe overleaf)
350g peas, broad beans and sprouting
  broccoli, steamed, to serve

Paupiette of Sole with Watercress Mousse

PAUPIETTE DE SOLE AU CRESSON

A paupiette is conventionally any thin slice of meat or fish rolled and stuffed with a filling, although in this case two delicate slices of sole are simply sandwiched together with a creamy herb mousse. The fresh colours and light flavours make for perfect fare on a warm summer's day.

Pick and wash the leaves from the watercress, parsley and baby spinach, removing most of the stalks.

Blanch the leaves in a pan of boiling salted water until just tender (approximately 30 seconds). Strain and refresh under cold running water, before gently squeezing out most of the water. In a liquidiser blend the leaves into a very fine purée.

Cut 12 of the sole fillets into equal sizes, approximately 10–12 cm in length, and set aside on a flat tray in the fridge. Dice the remaining two sole fillets and the leftover sole trimmings for the mousse, put them into a food processor bowl and chill in the fridge. When chilled, blend the sole in the processor with a good pinch of salt until it is very fine, making sure to scrape the sides of the bowl with a spatula from time to time.

Extra care must be taken to ensure that the fish mixture does not get too warm at any stage. Also, do not be tempted to omit the salt when blending the fish, as it helps to make the mousse finer.

Once the fish is completely smooth, add the herb purée and the raw egg and pulse well. Add the cream in three stages, also on the pulse setting. If desired the mousse can be passed through a sieve to make it even smoother before chilling again.

Lay out six of the sole fillets and season with salt and pepper, then spread the watercress mousse on to each of these fillets to a thickness of approximately 0.5 cm. Lay the remaining six fillets on top to create a sandwich effect, then carefully wrap each in plastic film, ensuring the ends are tied securely. Leave the sole paupiettes in the fridge for at least an hour.

In a wide pan of water warmed to around 70°C gently poach the sole fillets for 10–12 minutes. It is vital not to let the water rise above this temperature as the fish will then overcook, twist and shrink. Remove the film.

Serve on a pool of beurre blanc sauce (see right) accompanied by a panache of steamed green vegetables such as peas, broad beans and sprouting broccoli.

PRESENTATION

An individual Paupiette of Sole is here served on a more contemporary plate from the twentieth century – plain white, with gilded lines and a crown on the rim. This simple presentation accentuates the vivid contrast of the green vegetables against the clean white plate, allowing the summer colours of the dish to come to the fore.

❧ *When serving the paupiette, try to position it so the line of pale mousse is visible – heaps of vegetables over the top will obscure your delicate handiwork.*

Beurre Blanc Sauce

INGREDIENTS

3 tablespoons white wine vinegar
2 tablespoons white wine
2 shallots, peeled and roughly chopped
8–10 white peppercorns, lightly broken
1 sprig tarragon (or chervil), stalks only
2 tablespoons double cream
200g unsalted butter, diced

In a small saucepan, heat the vinegar and white wine with the chopped shallots, peppercorns and tarragon stalks until the liquid has almost completely evaporated.

Reduce the heat and add the cream, stirring continuously, then add the diced butter, a small amount at a time, allowing each amount to fully emulsify before adding more. It is crucial not to let the sauce get too hot; it must never boil.

Once you have added all the butter, the sauce should resemble a thin custard. Sieve the sauce to remove the shallots, peppercorns and tarragon. Adjust the seasoning to taste, and keep warm until required.

SERVES 6

INGREDIENTS

For the Sablé:

1 free-range egg yolk

45g unrefined caster sugar

50g softened unsalted butter

65g plain flour

1g fine sea salt

5g baking powder

For the lemon cream:

2 unwaxed lemons, zest and juice

70g unrefined caster sugar

3 free-range eggs, plus 1 free-range
    egg yolk

65g chilled unsalted butter, cut
    into cubes

2 250g punnets of English
    strawberries

EQUIPMENT

15cm cake tin

Sablé Breton with English Strawberries and Lemon Cream

SABLÉ BRETON AUX FRAISES

The Sablé Breton is a traditional butter biscuit from Brittany in France, but the addition here of strawberries and lemon cream turns it into something rather more English. It is remarkably straightforward to assemble but, once made, looks the absolute epitome of a sumptuous summer dessert.

Preheat the oven to 170°C (325°F, gas mark 3).

FOR THE SABLÉ BRETON

Prepare the cake tin by greasing with butter and lining the bottom with baking paper. Place the lined tin on to a flat, heavy-duty baking tray and leave to one side until required.

Whisk together the egg yolk and 40g of sugar in a bowl until light and fluffy. Add the softened butter and continue to whisk until a smooth paste is achieved. Sift together the flour, salt and baking powder, and fold into the egg mix until all ingredients are combined evenly. The paste should now feel quite firm.

Place the paste into the centre of the lined cake tin and, using the back of a metal spoon or a plastic spatula, spread evenly over the base of the tin.

Place on the middle shelf of the preheated oven and bake for approximately 12 minutes, or until the Sablé turns a light golden brown. Once baked, remove from the oven and allow to cool before removing the tin and the baking paper.

FOR THE LEMON CREAM

Put the lemon zest, lemon juice, 70g of sugar and the eggs and remaining egg yolk into a heatproof bowl. Sit the bowl over a saucepan of gently simmering water. Ensure that the water is not touching the bottom of the bowl.

Stir the mixture continuously until it begins to simmer.

Remove the bowl from the heat and slowly add the cubes of chilled butter. Stir until they have all melted into the lemon cream mixture.

Set aside to cool, covering immediately with plastic film to prevent a skin from forming. Chill and keep in the fridge until required.

To assemble the Sablé Breton

Place the Sablé Breton on to your serving plate and carefully spoon the lemon cream on to the sunken centre of the shortbread. Using a palette knife, spread the cream evenly over the surface, trying not to get any on the raised edges.

Remove the stalks and leaves from the strawberries, and, using a clean, damp kitchen towel, gently wipe the surface of each fruit. Carefully cut into quarters. Place each strawberry quarter on to the lemon cream with the cut side facing upwards; do this until all of the lemon cream is covered. For best results serve immediately.

Presentation

The Sablé Breton sits on an exceptionally decorative cake stand from the Rockingham Dessert Service. The Sablé is a bold dessert in itself, so can hold its own against elaborate chinaware.

The Rockingham service was commissioned by William IV, following his accession in 1830, from the Rockingham works in Yorkshire. The service originally consisted of 56 large decorative pieces and twelve dozen plates, and may confidently lay claim to be the most ambitious service ever produced by an English factory.

The Rockingham factory was founded in 1825 by the Brameld family and produced works of great quality. The design of the Rockingham service includes shells and coral celebrating the nation's maritime achievements (William IV, as Duke of Clarence, had served in the Royal Navy).

Exotic fruits such as pineapples and guavas, reproduced in brilliant colours, conjure up visions of Britain's overseas territories, although many of the pieces also include British landscapes, castles and country houses. The service was completed in 1837 and was first used at the Coronation Banquet of Queen Victoria in 1838. A selection from this service is displayed as part of the setting for a State Banquet in the Ballroom of Buckingham Palace, most recently for the visit of the President of the Republic of Korea in November 2013.

This summer lunch table has made use of a set of William IV glasses, delicately fluted and engraved with floral motifs. The pink-tinted wine glasses were added to this set by Queen Victoria in 1871, from Osler in Bond Street.

❦ Selecting flowers to tone with the colour of your glassware is an easy way to create a unified, but not uniform, impression.

Napkins, embroidered with the letter 'E' for 'Elizabeth', are displayed on a glass side plate over an intricate lace cloth, part of a set commissioned by The Queen in 1977 from the Irish Linen Company.

❦ Proper linen always adds a touch of elegance; layer table linens of different shades to create interest.

AUTUMN

Langoustines Lossiemouth

Partridge Hotpot

Rhubarb and White Chocolate Parfait

Autumn suppers demand comforting stews and casseroles — or, as here, a hotpot of flavourful partridge, topped with golden-brown potato. As a starter, langoustines are served in a bubbling cheese sauce; while pudding combines pink rhubarb and white chocolate for a last taste of summer.

Langoustines à la Lossiemouth

Hotpot au Perdreau

Parfait au Chocolat Blanc
et Rhubarbe

SERVES 6

INGREDIENTS

18 uncooked medium langoustines

600g baby spinach, washed

50g shallots, finely chopped

150g button mushrooms, sliced

150g diced tomato *concassé*
    (tomatoes peeled, deseeded and
    roughly chopped)

100g butter

10ml oil

2 teaspoons chopped tarragon

salt and pepper

For the Mornay sauce:

500ml milk

½ onion

1 bay leaf

1 clove

30g butter

30g plain flour

120g strong cheddar cheese, grated

Langoustines Lossiemouth

LANGOUSTINES À LA LOSSIEMOUTH

This is a very simple dish using one of Scotland's finest products – langoustines, or 'Dublin Bay prawns'. A pleasing appetiser on an autumn evening or an indulgent main course when you are in need of something more comforting.

Place the onion, bay leaf, clove and milk in a small pan and bring to the boil. Leave the milk to infuse for 15 minutes.

Melt the butter in a small, thick-bottomed pan. Add the flour and stir with a whisk; cook gently for 1–2 minutes. Strain the milk and slowly pour into the butter/flour mixture, whisking as you bring it towards the boil over a medium heat. As the sauce reaches the boil, lower the heat and cook gently for 10 minutes, stirring frequently. Check and adjust the seasoning before removing from the heat, then add most of the grated cheese. Cover and keep warm until ready to serve.

Heat a heavy-based pan, add the oil and melt in 50g of the butter. Wilt the baby spinach quickly in the pan, season; drain and keep warm in a serving dish.

In a frying pan gently sauté the shallots and langoustines in a little oil, without colouring, before adding the sliced mushrooms. Season and add the diced tomato *concassé* and tarragon. Place the langoustine mixture neatly on to the spinach and coat with the Mornay sauce. Sprinkle with the remainder of the grated cheese and glaze under the grill until lightly coloured.

PRESENTATION

Here we have opted to present individual portions of the Langoustines Lossiemouth. These little two-handled copper pans sit on plates from a dinner service presented to The Queen by the President of Portugal, General Craveiro Lopes, during a State Visit to the United Kingdom in October 1955. All the plates carry an EIIR cypher and are decorated with inlaid gold patterns of the York rose, thistle and shamrock, symbols of the kingdoms of England, Scotland and Ireland.

To prepare the six portions individually, divide the spinach between six oven-proof dishes and lay the langoustine mixture and mornay sauce on top of each.

SERVES 6

INGREDIENTS

1kg potatoes

4 oven-ready partridges (the red-
  legged, or French, variety)

2 tablespoons vegetable oil

salt and pepper

400g top quality sausage meat, rolled
  into 12 balls

1 onion, chopped

2 carrots, peeled, washed and cut
  into 2cm pieces

2 leeks, trimmed, washed and cut
  into 2cm pieces

25g butter

150ml dry cider

3–4 sprigs of thyme

1 bay leaf

300ml game or chicken stock

Partridge Hotpot

HOTPOT AU PERDREAU

Partridge season in Britain runs from September through to the start of February; of the two main types of partridge available here, we would usually use the larger and milder red-legged (or French) partridge for this dish. These are more commonly available than the native grey partridge.

Preheat the oven to 180°C (350°F, gas mark 4).

Peel and cut the potatoes into 0.75cm-thick slices and parboil in a large pan of lightly salted water. Drain well and cut into circles using a small round cutter.

Heat 1 tablespoon of the oil in a heavy flameproof casserole dish. Season the partridges with salt and black pepper and fry over a medium heat for 2–4 minutes, turning, until well browned all over. Transfer to a plate and set aside. Do the same with the sausage meat, again removing to a plate after frying, and then add the onion, carrots and leeks and remaining oil. Gently soften the vegetables without allowing them to gain too much colour (around 5 minutes).

Whilst the vegetables are cooking, cut the legs from the partridges, and then slice the breast meat away from the remaining bone. (You can reserve the carcasses for making stock or soup.)

Add the cider, thyme and bay leaf to the casserole and bring to the boil before slowly stirring in the stock. When the casserole has returned to the boil add the partridge and sausage meat, adjusting the seasoning to taste. Cover the mixture with overlapping slices of potato and dot with butter. Bake in the oven for 20–30 minutes until the potatoes are tender and golden brown.

PRESENTATION

The Partridge Hotpot photographed here is fresh out of the oven, still in two copper pans. Such pans, lined with tin, are still used in both the kitchens of Buckingham Palace and Windsor Castle; some date back as far as the reigns of George IV or Queen Victoria. They are easily identifiable by the royal crests, engraved on the copper.

The hotpot will break up if you attempt to transfer it to a separate serving dish, so allow your diners to admire the inviting golden layer of potatoes by bringing the casserole to the table straight from the oven.

SERVES 6

INGREDIENTS

300g fresh rhubarb

seeds from ⅓ of a fresh vanilla pod

1 free-range egg yolk

35g caster sugar

100g semi-whipped whipping cream*

12 discs of chocolate meringue sponge
  (see p. 68), cut to fit the rings

300g white chocolate

lustre dust

EQUIPMENT

6 individual plastic or metal rings,
  6cm width, 3.5cm depth

12 acetate strips

disposable piping bags

paintbrush for lustre dust

* To achieve semi-whipped whipping
  cream, whip the cream until it only
  just forms soft peaks.

Rhubarb and White Chocolate Parfait

PARFAIT AU CHOCOLAT BLANC ET RHUBARBE

This is an impressively sophisticated dessert. The combination of chocolate and rhubarb is a slightly uncommon but nevertheless delectable pairing – the tart flavour of the fruit counterbalanced by the rich sweetness of white chocolate.

First place the rings on to a flat tray lined with baking paper. Place a strip of acetate into each ring; put to one side.

Wash the rhubarb and chop into 1cm pieces. Place the rhubarb, the vanilla seeds and 20g of the sugar into a saucepan and gently warm until the rhubarb has softened. This will help to extract some of the juices. Set aside two thirds of the rhubarb for the garnish; blend the remaining third in a processor to create a purée. Pass the purée through a sieve to make it smooth. Set to one side to cool.

Whisk the egg yolk and the remaining 15g of sugar in a round-bottomed bowl until they become pale and fluffy. Add to this your purée, before finally folding in the semi-whipped whipping cream. At this point ensure the rhubarb parfait is sweet enough for your taste; more sugar can be added if required.

At the base of a ring place a chocolate meringue sponge disc, then spoon or pipe the parfait mixture to one-third of the way up the ring. Place the second sponge disc on top and then pipe to the top of the ring with parfait mix. Do so for all six rings, and then carefully place the tray into the freezer for at least an hour, preferably overnight. Once frozen, remove the rings and acetate strips.

TO ASSEMBLE THE PARFAIT

First cut acetate strips to the required length and width to wrap around each iced parfait. Using the paintbrush and lustre dust, decorate the acetate strips as you desire – a few brush strokes will usually suffice.

Melt the white chocolate either in a microwave or in a bowl over a saucepan of simmering water, heating gently until the chocolate has only just melted.

Using a spoon, pour some of the white chocolate on to a dusted strip; exchange the spoon for a small palette knife and carefully spread the chocolate evenly over the entire piece of acetate. Gently pick up the acetate and wrap around the frozen parfait, with the chocolate facing inwards to the parfait. Repeat for all six parfaits and return to the freezer to set fully.

Remove the parfaits from the freezer 20–30 minutes before serving; peel off the acetate strips. When you are ready to serve, place each parfait on the centre of a plate and garnish with the remaining poached rhubarb. For a more extravagant occasion you could also add some curls of white chocolate, sprigs of mint and cubes of champagne jelly.

PRESENTATION

The pretty pinks and cream of the delicate parfait suit an equally pretty plate: in this case we have selected a piece from the Staffordshire Minton Dessert Service, made for Queen Victoria in 1879. Its turquoise border is a bright counterpoise to the reds and browns of autumn. Hidden beneath the parfait is an emblem depicting the royal monogram V&A – Victoria and Albert.

Chocolate Meringue Sponge

(FOR USE IN THE RHUBARB AND WHITE CHOCOLATE PARFAIT)

This incredibly simple sponge is the perfect base for the rhubarb parfait.
It can be made the day before and stored in an airtight container overnight.
Use the parfait rings (metal or plastic) as cutters or templates when it comes
to preparing the discs of sponge.

SERVES 6

INGREDIENTS

3 free-range eggs, separated
50g unrefined caster sugar
20g extra brute cocoa powder
   (cocoa powder with a high
   cocoa content mass), sieved

EQUIPMENT

1 flat Swiss roll tin

Preheat the oven to 170°C (325°F, gas mark 3). Grease a flat Swiss roll tin and then line with baking paper.

Whisk the egg whites, gradually adding the caster sugar a little at a time, until the mixture stands up in peaks when the whisk is lifted. This mixture will form a stiff meringue base.

Remove the whisk from the mixture and gently fold in the egg yolks. Finally fold in the sieved cocoa powder until fully combined.

Carefully spread the meringue mixture evenly across a flat Swiss roll tin.

Place in the oven and bake until the sponge springs back into shape when pressed with a finger, approximately 7–10 minutes. Times will vary depending on the oven.

Once baked and removed from the oven, immediately turn the sponge out on to another sheet of baking paper, and allow to cool.

Set aside until needed for the parfait.

The chocolate meringue sponge recipe can also be used simply for a chocolate swiss roll or yule log at Christmas.

Cups of coffee served with petits fours are a sophisticated conclusion to a meal. These dainty little cups and saucers are part of a silver-gilt coffee service presented to King George V on his Coronation in 1911 by King Haakon VII and Queen Maud of Norway; they are deocrated with blue *guilloché* enamel.

A table setting for an intimate dinner party. Here the setting is the Chinese Dining Room. The interior of the Chinese Dining Room includes some of the original fittings from the Brighton Pavilion, which were used to decorate rooms on the East Front of the palace in the new wing added by Queen Victoria in 1847. Originally this room served as her Luncheon Room. The table-setting here has been kept relatively simple, with no tablecloth to hide the quality of the polished table and using only a few centre table displays with flowers and shaded candelabras to complement the elaborate and exotic decoration of the room.

Fresh, perfectly ripe fruit is always welcome as a simple and economical way to end a rich meal. Traditionally this was known as 'Dessert Service', and was served after the pudding course. At Buckingham Palace cheese is not normally served after dinner, but fruit is still provided, with china and cutlery prepared as shown here. The plates – in this case three late eighteenth-century Sèvres soft paste porcelain plates – each hold a Brierley crystal finger bowl, on a linen doily, with a fruit knife, fork and spoon. These are placed in front of each guest, who should remove the cutlery and place the finger bowl on the doily in front of their plate. The fruit is then offered to the guest who has everything they need to enjoy it without getting their fingers sticky.

Winter

Arbroath Smokie, Leek and Courgette Tart

Roasted Loin of Balmoral Venison

Apricot Crêpes Soufflé

A starter of smoked fish, a roast loin of venison and
comforting crêpes provide a satisfying winter feast
for a dinner party to celebrate the end of the year.
Strong, earthy flavours and rich, warm colours lure
us in out of the cold.

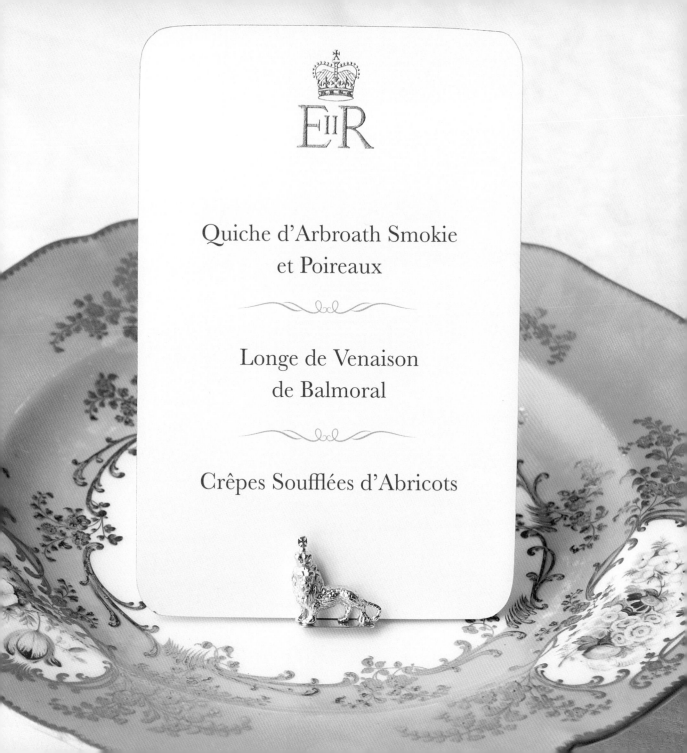

EⁱIR

Quiche d'Arbroath Smokie
et Poireaux

Longe de Venaison
de Balmoral

Crêpes Soufflées d'Abricots

Serves 8

Ingredients

For the pastry:

120g plain flour

1 pinch salt

60g butter, chilled and diced into
small cubes

1 free-range egg

2–4 tablespoons iced water

For the filling:

2 Arbroath smokies (or other
good quality smoked haddocks,
minimum 500g)

125ml milk

125ml double cream

1 clove garlic

2 large sprigs thyme

around 10 peppercorns

1 bay leaf

60ml olive oil

150g courgettes

200g leeks

salt and pepper

2 free-range eggs, beaten

Equipment

1 20cm flan tin

Arbroath Smokie, Leek and Courgette Tart

QUICHE D'ARBROATH SMOKIE ET POIREAUX

Arbroath smokies are hot-smoked haddocks, only produced in the area
around the town of Arbroath in Scotland, from where they are transported
to suppliers across Britain.

Preheat the oven to 180°C (350°F, gas mark 4).
Grease the flan ring.

TO MAKE THE SAVOURY PASTRY

Place the flour, salt and cold diced butter on to a
clean dry work surface and rub the butter into the
flour with the tips of your fingers until a fine crumb
is achieved. Add the egg and continue to work the
dough, adding the water a little at a time to make
the pastry soft, but not sticky. It is important that
you do not overwork the dough at this stage.

Form the dough into a flattened ball, wrap in
greaseproof paper and refrigerate for at least an
hour to rest. (Do not omit the resting time or your
pastry will shrink when you cook it.)

After resting, roll out the dough to the desired
thickness (approximately 0.5cm) and use it to line
the greased flan tin, leaving an overhang of about
1 cm around the edges. Prick the pastry lightly
with a fork and allow the lined tin to rest in the
fridge for a further 30 minutes.

Blind bake the tart with baking beans at 180°C
for about 20 minutes, until a light golden colour.
Allow to rest for a few minutes before removing the
baking beans. Turn the oven temperature down to
150°C (300°F, gas mark 2).

Gently poach the fish in the milk and cream for
4–5 minutes with half the garlic and thyme, the
peppercorns and the bay leaf. Allow the fish to cool
in the mixture before removing from the liquid
(reserve liquid for use later in the custard).

Remove the skin from the fish and flake the flesh into a clean bowl, taking care to discard any bones (there are a lot of very small bones in a smokie).

Wash and trim the courgettes, cut in half lengthwise, then cut into slices 0.25cm thick. Lightly sauté the courgettes in the olive oil with the remaining garlic and thyme, and season with salt and pepper. When just cooked, remove the garlic and thyme. Set aside the courgettes.

Carefully wash and trim the leeks, keeping most of the green; slice thinly and sauté in the same way as the courgettes.

Gently mix the Arbroath smokie together with the courgettes and the leeks.

TO MAKE THE CUSTARD

Strain the milk and cream mixture through a strainer. Whisk in the two beaten eggs and adjust the seasoning.

Gently add the fish and vegetable filling to the tart base and spread it out evenly. Pour over the custard, and cook in the oven at 150°C for 30 minutes. When the custard is just set but still slightly wobbly, take it out of the oven and allow it to sit for 15 minutes – or as long as temptation permits – before trimming the overlapping pastry and serving.

PRESENTATION

The tart makes a substantial starter or alternatively a light lunch or supper. Here we have served it on a plain white china plate with a gold rim, but added in a different texture by placing it on to a larger pewter dish. Sometimes items found outside the kitchen or dining room (these pewter plates were sat above a fireplace) can provide an unexpected finishing touch.

Set to the side of the tart are a decanter and glasses from a set known as the Prince Regent Service (or Warrington Service), which dates from 1806 to 1811. The then-Prince of Wales (the future George IV) attended a dinner given by the Corporation of Liverpool, and admired the glass service in use that evening. The Prince asked the Mayor of Liverpool to order him a few dozen glasses. Instead the Mayor ordered a full service, comprising over 300 pieces, including claret and port glasses, decanters, coolers, carafes, water jug and finger bowls, all engraved with the Prince of Wales's feathers, and presented the service to the Prince as a gift.

SERVES 6

INGREDIENTS
1 loin of venison (1–1.5kg)
2 cloves of garlic
2 sprigs of thyme
50g unsalted butter
50ml vegetable oil
salt and pepper

For the sauce:
300g shallots, peeled and chopped
200g carrots, peeled and chopped
10 juniper berries
1 clove of garlic, crushed
1 large sprig of thyme
30ml sherry vinegar
100g redcurrant jelly
200ml port
800ml venison stock (if unavailable,
    use beef stock)

1 kg Scottish girolles, to serve
Pink fir potatoes, to serve

Roasted Loin of Balmoral Venison

LONGE DE VENAISON DE BALMORAL

The venison from the Balmoral Estate is from the larger red deer rather than roe or fallow. The royal kitchens prefer this for the more gamey flavour acquired from grazing on Highland vegetation.

Ask your butcher to prepare the loin by taking off the fillets, removing any sinews and chopping the carcass (should you have the time to make your own stock).

Preheat the oven to 100°C (225°F, gas mark ¼).

Fry any leftover trimmings from the loin in a little oil in a heavy-based pan until golden brown and beginning to caramelise. Add in the roughly chopped shallots, carrots, juniper berries, garlic and thyme. Stir well to combine, and allow to colour slightly before de-glazing the pan with the sherry vinegar and a spatula, taking care to release any of the tasty morsels sticking to the pan.

Add the redcurrant jelly and allow it to coat all the ingredients in the pan, but do not allow it to colour. Pour in the port and reduce the mixture by two thirds. Pour in the venison stock, bring to the boil and skim off any residue that rises to the surface. Allow to simmer and reduce gently for around 40 minutes. Strain the sauce and reserve until just before you are ready to serve.

Season the loin of venison with salt and pepper. In a hot pan with a little oil, fry the seasoned loin until sealed all over. Add the 2 cloves of extra garlic and thyme and transfer to the oven to roast for approximately 25 minutes if you like your venison pink; longer if you so wish.

Allow the meat to rest in a warm place for ten minutes before serving with the sauce, some Scottish girolles sautéed in butter, and beautifully simple boiled Pink Fir potatoes.

PRESENTATION

The Loin of Venison is presented on a wooden carving board, ready to be carved and served on to the white porcelain plates to the side. The colours of this dish – from the crimson of the meat to the greens of the cabbage – make a plain setting preferable, although the gilt scalloped edging of these plates is appropriate to the richness of the food. These plates are part of the Guards Dinner Service from Royal Worcester, presented to The Queen and the Duke of Edinburgh by all the Foot Guard Regiments (apart from the Grenadier Guards) in 1947 as a wedding present. The emblem visible on the rim is the Guards' Star.

❧ Berries and coloured foliage can be a readily available alternative to flowers for the table in winter. The rich colours of the winter leaves chime well with the dark venison.

The venison is pictured (right) with the orange girolles and a pan of freshly steamed cabbage. The sauce and a pot of horseradish complete the arrangement.

SERVES 6

INGREDIENTS

35g plain flour

2 free-range eggs, separated, plus
  1 whole free-range egg

20g melted unsalted butter, plus
  30g butter to assemble the crêpes
  once cooked

40ml full-fat milk

35g unrefined caster sugar

190ml double cream

200g apricot preserve

EQUIPMENT

10cm flan moulds or non-stick blini
  pans, 2 or 3 per person; or 2 x 15cm
  cake tins*

* If you do not have the flan moulds or
  blini pans, bake the soufflé mixture in
  2 x 15cm cake tins for 10–15 minutes.
  Proceed as in the method, stacking the
  two crêpes on top of each other. Cut
  wedges to serve.

Apricot Crêpes Soufflé

CRÊPES SOUFFLÉES D'ABRICOTS

Somewhere between a fluffy soufflé and a pancake, these fabulous desserts combine the best of both.

Preheat the oven to 180°C (350°F, gas mark 4).

Prepare the flan moulds or blini pans by greasing with butter and placing on to a flat baking tray. Put this into the oven whilst you prepare the soufflé batter.

Sift the flour. Prepare the soufflé batter by mixing together the whole egg, two egg yolks, melted butter, milk, half the sugar, the cream and finally the flour. Whisk the batter until smooth and place to one side.

Whisk the two egg whites with the remaining sugar until they form light peaks that support themselves; gently fold them through the batter, combining them fully.

Once the oven has reached the correct temperature, carefully remove the flat baking tray. Pour the soufflé mixture into the flan moulds (or blini pans).

Return the tray to the oven and bake for 5–8 minutes, or until the soufflé is golden brown in appearance.

Whilst the crêpes soufflé are baking, prepare the apricot sauce to accompany the dessert. Melt the 30g of butter. In a separate saucepan, gently warm the apricot preserve, adding a little water if required to amend the consistency: it should be a thick enough syrup to coat the crêpes.

Once the crêpes soufflé are ready, work quickly to remove them from the oven and then from their moulds. Using a palette knife or plastic spatula, place the first crêpe on to your serving dishes, then with a cocktail stick pierce a few holes in the crêpe – this will allow the crêpes soufflé to absorb the butter and apricot jam that you will spoon over.

Repeat this process until three crêpes are placed on top of each other on each serving dish. Spoon the jam over the crêpes and allow it to pour down the sides and on to the dishes.

PRESENTATION

The crêpes soufflé are served here on a selection of Coalport dessert plates. These were purchased by Queen Victoria through Coalport's agent, Daniells of New Bond Street, at various times in the mid-nineteenth century. The plates come in a selection of jewel-vivid hues – a welcome splash in a wintry meal – and show how this dessert can be set against a variety of different colours.

❧ A small sprig of mint and a slice of tinned apricot adds the finishing touch to the top of the crêpes.

SPRING

Eggs Drumkilbo

Cutlet of Windsor Lamb with Sauce Paloise

Blackcurrant Sorbet

Spring, and the larder is filled with fresh produce and seasonal delicacies. One of The Queen Mother's favourite dishes features in this menu, together with the finest spring lamb, lightly dressed and grilled. A delicious sorbet provides a spectacular end to the meal.

Oeufs Drumkilbo

Cotelettes d'Agneau de Windsor

Sorbet aux Cassis

SERVES 4

INGREDIENTS

3 hard-boiled eggs

75g peeled prawns

3 plum tomatoes, peeled, deseeded
   and diced

chervil leaves for decoration

2 500g Scottish lobsters

100ml clear fish stock

3 gelatine leaves

100g mayonnaise

25ml ketchup

a splash of anchovy essence

a splash of Worcestershire sauce

10g parsley, blanched and chopped

chopped chives

salt and pepper

*It is quite possible to use halved quails'
eggs (as pictured) as a topping, in place of
the sliced hens' eggs.*

Eggs Drumkilbo

OEUFS DRUMKILBO

Eggs Drumkilbo is famous as a dish particularly enjoyed by Queen Elizabeth The Queen Mother. The name originates from an ancient Highland estate in Perthshire, Drumkilbo, where the dish was supposedly created. It is a marvellous mix of the decadent and the everyday – with little chunks of lobster and prawn joined by mayonnaise and ketchup, and the whole mixture crowned with a jewel-like slice of egg.

Soak the gelatine leaves in ice-cold water to soften.

Cut two of the eggs into thin slices (enough for one per person), and top each slice with a single prawn, a lozenge of tomato and a small piece of chervil. Reserve these slices on a plate.

Chop the lobster and prawns into 0.5cm pieces, and place in a large bowl. Dice the remaining egg and add to the shellfish, along with the diced tomato.

Warm the fish stock to just below boiling point. Squeeze dry the soaked gelatine leaves and stir into the stock. When the gelatine is entirely dissolved, remove the stock from the heat.

Mix together the mayonnaise, ketchup, anchovy essence, Worcestershire sauce and a third of the fish stock (reserving the remainder for the aspic garnish). Gently fold this sauce into the shellfish and egg mixture; add the herbs and adjust the seasoning. Neatly spoon the mixture into your serving dish (or each individual serving dish, as pictured), and smooth the top with a palette knife.

Chill in the fridge for an hour before glazing with the remaining aspic (gelatine-stock mixture) and then return to the fridge to set the glaze. Before serving, decorate with the egg slices.

PRESENTATION

Eggs Drumkilbo are served at a variety of occasions. Here the wonderful ingredients of this dish are served in an elegant but simple glass dish and liner. These glasses are from Leerdam and were a wedding gift to The Queen and Prince Philip from the Government and people of the Netherlands in 1947. They sit on a beautifully ornate plate from Royal Worcester, made by the Kerr & Binns factory for Queen Victoria, part of a set commissioned in 1860. The artist was Thomas Bott and the service was displayed at the International Exhibition at the South Kensington Museum (now the V&A) in 1862.

Sitting behind the Eggs Drumkilbo is a decorative cut-glass and gilt basket, filled here with soft-boiled quails' eggs – still in their exquisite mottled shells. At other times this basket might be filled with other foods – it is one of a set of four bonbon baskets dated to 1843, believed to have been purchased by Queen Victoria. You can just see the little crown at the top of the handle.

This photograph was taken in the White Drawing Room at Buckingham Palace.

SERVES 6

INGREDIENTS

12 cutlets of lamb (French-trimmed)

100ml herb oil (see p. 98)

36 spears of English asparagus

750g Jersey Royal new potatoes

30g butter

salt and pepper

For the sauce:

1 small bunch mint

350ml white wine vinegar

1 teaspoon white peppercorns

100g shallots, finely chopped

250g unsalted butter

3 free-range egg yolks

a squeeze of lemon juice

Cutlets of Windsor Lamb with Sauce Paloise

COTELETTES D'AGNEAU DE WINDSOR

Perfect for a sunny springtime lunch, this dish utilises some of the finest British produce, at its best during this time of year. We would use spring lamb from the Windsor Estate, and English asparagus – usually arriving in shops in late April – which is simply beyond compare.

Pick the leaves from the mint and set aside. Chop the mint stalks, then combine with the vinegar, peppercorns and shallots in a pan. Bring to the boil over a high heat and then continue to cook until the mixture has reduced by two-thirds.

Blanch the mint leaves in boiling water for 10–15 seconds to soften, then quickly refresh under cold running water. Gently squeeze the leaves dry and finely chop with a sharp knife.

Melt the butter in a pan, skimming off any white solids that rise to the surface. Keep warm until you are ready to make the sauce.

In a heatproof bowl placed over a pan of simmering water, whisk together the egg yolks and the vinegar reduction until they form a pale yellow foam (sabayon) which should hold its shape when you lift the whisk. (You must ensure that the sabayon does not get too hot or the egg yolk will start to cook.)

Slowly trickle the warm butter into the sabayon with a ladle, whisking all the time. The sauce should acquire a consistency similar to that of mayonnaise. Add a squeeze of lemon juice and the chopped blanched mint.

Carefully peel and trim the asparagus, taking care to remove the woody stems at the base of the spears.

Wash the Jersey Royals well and bring to the boil in a large pan of salted water. Turn down the heat until the pan is just simmering and allow to cook gently until tender. Once the potatoes are cooked, strain them and return to the heat briefly to dry off, before adding a knob of butter.

Cover and keep somewhere warm for at least 10 minutes before serving: this is so the potatoes can really absorb the butter.

Season the lamb cutlets with sea salt, freshly milled pepper and the herb oil before grilling in a hot griddle pan for 3–5 minutes per side (depending on how you like your lamb cooked).

Allow the lamb to sit and rest somewhere warm for five minutes. In the meantime, cook the asparagus in boiling salted water for 4–5 minutes, depending on the thickness of the spears. Serve the lamb with the asparagus, Jersey Royals and a generous pot of warm sauce paloise.

PRESENTATION

The lamb cutlets are arranged on an oval platter, surrounded by ornate dishes from the Marcolini Dresden King's Service, dated between 1774 and 1814. A little porcelain putto gazes down at the feast from his perch on the lid of the vegetable dish. To add to the drama of the setting, the claret for the lamb is served from one of a pair of flattened, oval-cut, glass and silver gilt claret jugs by Charles Edwards, dated 1891 to 1892, and again believed to have been purchased by Queen Victoria.

Herb Oil

You can make this infused oil with any herbs that you especially like or happen to have available. If you wish to give it a more intense flavour you can blend the herbs and the oil in a food processor once it has been heated, which is lovely served on pasta or for cooking a whole baked fish.

INGREDIENTS

500ml olive oil
2 cloves of garlic, lightly broken
½ bunch thyme
½ bunch rosemary
1 large sprig of basil
a few good sprigs of marjoram

Lightly bruise the herbs and garlic before putting them into a saucepan with the oil. Heat very gently, allowing the herbs to infuse for around 10–15 minutes. Do not allow the oil to get too hot as the herbs must not start to fry. Once the oil has warmed through, remove it from the heat and leave the herbs in it overnight (or for as long as possible) before straining the oil. You can use the herbs in a marinade for a Sunday roast.

SERVES 6

INGREDIENTS
140ml water
150g unrefined caster sugar
40g liquid glucose
500g blackcurrants (fresh or frozen)

EQUIPMENT
Ice cream maker (non-essential)

Blackcurrant Sorbet

SORBET AUX CASSIS

A sorbet is a wonderful way to preserve the vibrant tang of these delicious fruits – and the perfect dessert to have tucked away in the freezer, ready to brighten the end of any meal.

To make the sorbet syrup, put the water, sugar and glucose into a saucepan and bring to a gentle simmer over a low heat.

Place the blackcurrants in a saucepan and gently warm. This will help to extract some of the juices. Once the fruit is fully softened, blend in a processor to create a purée. Pass the purée through a sieve into a bowl.

Add the syrup to the blackcurrant purée and mix well, using a spoon rather than a whisk. Check that the sorbet mixture is sweetened to your taste.

Set aside to cool, covering with plastic film to prevent a skin from forming on the surface.

Pour the sorbet mix into the ice cream machine and churn until you have a thick and creamy consistency throughout (the length of time required will depend on your machine). Store in the freezer until required. Serve with a few blackcurrants scattered across the top.

If you do not have an ice cream maker, you can whisk the sorbet mixture by hand. After cooling, pour the mixture into a shallow freezer dish. Place into the freezer. Remove and beat the mixture three to four times as it freezes.

Before serving, remove from the freezer and allow to thaw for around 10 minutes. Decorate each serving with a scattering of whole blackcurrants.

PRESENTATION

The Blackcurrant Sorbet is presented on one of a pair of silver-gilt stands with matching jelly or ice cream cups. Dated 1820 to 1821, by Philip Rundell of Rundell, Bridge and Rundell, they were purchased by George IV in July 1824 at a cost of £275 16s 10d. This was the last period when ice cream was such a fashionable part of the dessert course and by the 1840s, ice-cream coolers and their accompanying cups and stands were rarely manufactured. This was partly because of changing tastes; as dining styles changed, so did the demand for different elements of dining services. However, any small cups (and of course they need not be matching – teacups, small glasses) will suit this sweetly simple dessert.

❧ To achieve the swirling effect pictured here, you can pipe the slightly softened sorbet through a wide piping nozzle, or alternatively swirl in an upwards spiral using a fork.

Spring sunshine streams through the window, which on this side of Buckingham Palace overlooks the private garden. White and yellow roses from the Palace rose garden have been gathered in an informal arrangement at the centre of the table.

This menu is set within the grandeur of the White Drawing Room at Buckingham Palace and complements the setting with equally elaborate table decorations and accoutrements.

As for all royal menus, wines are carefully chosen to match the dishes. For this menu the white wine chosen is a Pouilly Fumé, Laroche Blanche, Domaine Laporte 2008. The Claret is Chateau Chasse Spleen 1996, and to accompany the blackcurrant sorbet, a champagne Pol Roger Blancs de Blancs 2000 is served.

The highly polished rosewood table gives us the opportunity to use fine linen table mats. The ones used here, together with the napkins, were a gift to The Queen and The Duke of Edinburgh in 1954 from the people of Malta. They consist of exquisite Gozo lacework, with the Garter Star represented in the lace.

The cutlery is silver-gilt, and forms part of a number of gilt services purchased by George IV. The decoration of this set, made between 1817 and 1820, depicts the honeysuckle plant and is hallmarked 'Paul Storr'. The crystal glasses are from the Garter Service, dating from various periods of the nineteenth century, with the Garter Badge as the main motif. The large cruets (for condiments) in front of each placesetting are lion-headed cruets from the reign of William IV.

SERVES 8

INGREDIENTS

225g McVitie's Rich Tea biscuits
115g softened unsalted butter
115g unrefined caster sugar
115g chopped dark chocolate
   (minimum 53% cocoa solids)
2 tablespoons warm water, or dark
   rum if you prefer

For the chocolate ganache:
125g dark chocolate, chopped
125g whipping cream

EQUIPMENT

15cm metal cake ring

Chocolate Biscuit Cake

Famous for being one of two royal wedding cakes to celebrate the marriage of the Duke and Duchess of Cambridge in 2011, this is a marvellously easy but nevertheless completely delicious 'cake', which requires absolutely no baking. You can decorate it in any way you wish; this recipe supplies the instructions for a simple ganache which makes the perfect base for more extravagant adornment.

Prepare the metal cake ring by greasing with butter and lining the sides and the bottom with baking paper. Place the lined ring on to a flat tray and leave to one side until required.

Break the biscuits into small pieces, around 1–2 cm in size. Do not place into a processor – the biscuits should not become crumbs.

Place the softened butter and the sugar into a bowl and cream together until light and fluffy.

Melt the chocolate either in the microwave or over a simmering saucepan of water. Once melted, pour the chocolate on to the butter and sugar and mix thoroughly. Finally, add the water or rum and then the broken biscuit pieces. Stir well to make sure that all the biscuit pieces are coated with the chocolate mix.

Place the mixture into the lined cake ring and carefully but firmly push it down to create an even texture. Place the cake into the fridge to chill until the chocolate becomes firm. This could take up to 30 minutes.

FOR THE CHOCOLATE GANACHE

To prepare the ganache for the cake covering, place the chopped chocolate into a bowl and pour the whipping cream into a saucepan. Bring the cream to a simmer and then pour over the chopped chocolate. Carefully stir until the chocolate has completely melted and the ganache is smoothly blended.

Remove the chocolate biscuit cake from the fridge and from the cake ring. Place on to a wire rack with a tray beneath to collect the excess ganache.

Carefully coat the chocolate biscuit cake with the warm ganache, making sure that all of the cake is evenly coated. Allow to set fully before moving to your service plate and decorating as desired.

PRESENTATION

Because this cake involves no baking, the ingredients can easily be increased proportionately to make larger sizes. It is also an excellent cake for stacking – this picture shows a 15cm cake on top of a 20cm cake, with the two tiers then decorated in chocolate ganache.

This two-tier version of the chocolate biscuit cake has been decorated with chocolate buttons and a chocolate royal coat of arms. The chocolate buttons were made using real footman's buttons taken from Royal Household uniforms; these were used to create moulds into which melted dark and milk chocolate was poured. Some of the buttons were then brushed with gold lustre dust to varying degrees, so that some appear completely gold and others merely glint.

Using chocolate buttons of different types and sizes is an easy way to embellish a plain chocolate cake; lustre dust can add a further element of sparkle and sophistication. You can even buy material to make original chocolate moulds at home, and use buttons or anything else you should wish to create your very own unique decorations.

Weights and Measures

OVEN TEMPERATURES

°C	°F	Gas mark
110	225	¼
130	250	½
140	275	1
150	300	2
170	325	3
180	350	4
190	375	5
200	400	6
220	425	7
230	450	8
240	475	9

AMERICAN WEIGHTS AND MEASURES CONVERSION CHART

	Metric	Imperial	US
Flour/Cocoa	25g	1oz	¼ cup
	50g	2oz	½ cup
	75g	3oz	¾ cup
	100g	4oz	1 cup
	120g	4½oz	1 cup
Butter/Sugar	25g	1oz	2 tbsp
	50g	2oz	¼ cup
	100g	4oz	½ cup
	175g	6oz	¾ cup
	225g	8oz	1 cup
Grated cheese	100g	4oz	1 cup

CAKE TIN SIZING CHART

cm	inches
15cm	6 inch
18cm	7 inch
20cm	8 inch
23cm	9 inch
25cm	10 inch

EGGS

All eggs used are large sized and free-range

Picture Credits

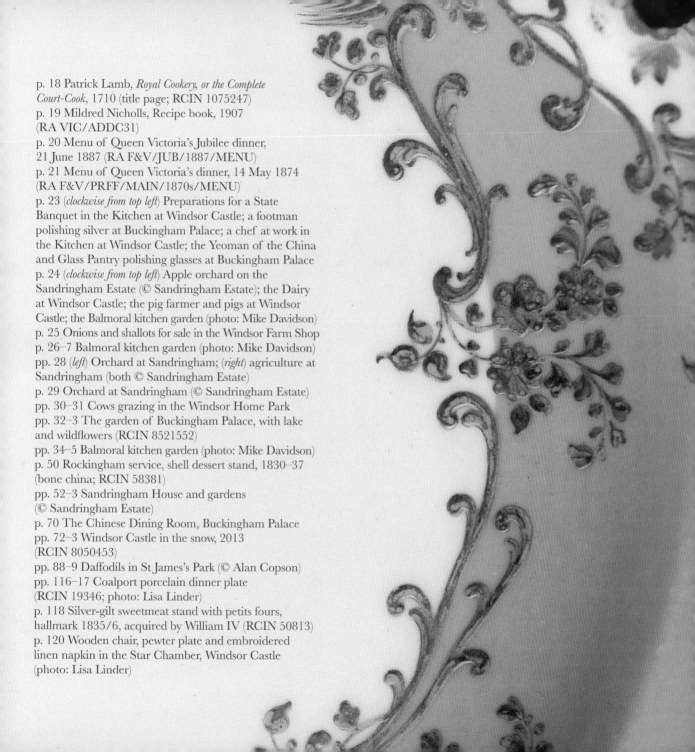

Acknowledgements

We are grateful to Her Majesty The Queen for permission to produce this book.

In putting together *A Royal Cookbook* we have been assisted by many of our colleagues from across the Royal Household. Our thanks firstly go to all of the kitchen team, particularly to Mark Fromont, Kathryn Cuthbertson and Giuliano Vilardo. Thanks are also due to Stephen Murray, Yeoman of the Silver and Gilt Pantry, and Stephen Marshall, Yeoman of the China and Glass Pantry, and their teams for the work on the historical information on the pieces chosen for this book, as well as to Kathryn Jones and Sally Goodsir from Royal Collection Trust for their curatorial expertise. We would like to express further gratitude to the following: Linda Saunders, Head Housekeeper at Buckingham Palace, and Rachel Gordon, Housekeeper at Windsor Castle, and their Linen Room staff; Diane Roberts, Assistant Florist, for her evocative flower arrangements; Richard Thompson, Palace Foreman, and his team for the photographic set-ups at Buckingham Palace; and Michael Devlin for the set-ups at Windsor Castle.

Finally we would like to thank Lisa Linder and Cynthia Inions for creating such superb photographs, Briony Hartley for her wonderful designs, and the publications team of Nina Chang and Jacky Colliss Harvey.

Published 2014 by Royal Collection Trust
York House
St James's Palace
London SW1A 1BQ

Reprinted 2014

**Find out more about the Royal Collection
and Palaces at www.royalcollection.org.uk
Subscribe to Royal Collection Trust's
e-Newsletter at
www.royalcollection.org.uk/newsletter**

ISBN 978 1 905686 78 0

014850

British Library Cataloguing in Publication data:
A catalogue record of this book is available from
the British Library.

Food photography by Lisa Linder
Food styling by Cynthia Inions
Designed by Goldust Design
Project Editor Nina Chang
Production Manager Debbie Wayment

Typeset in Baskerville and Trajan
Printed on Gardmat 150gsm
Colour reproduction by Altaimage, London
Printed and bound in Slovenia by Gorenjski tisk